Ten Generations

of

Byrds

in America

From Virginia to Alabama and Back

by Manuel H. Johnson, Jr.

CRUCE SPES MEA

This book is dedicated to the sons of Marietta Byrd and Henderson Franklin Johnson and their families.

www.mascotbooks.com

Ten Generations of Byrds in America: From Virginia to Alabama and Back

For more information, please contact:
Mascot Books
560 Herndon Parkway #120
Herndon, VA 20170
info@mascotbooks.com

Library of Congress Control Number: 2016919384

CPSIA Code: PBANG0117A
ISBN: 978-1-68401-131-5

Printed in the United States

TABLE OF CONTENTS

Preface

This genealogical study is focused primarily on my direct line of Byrd ancestors, beginning with the first immigrant to America and proceeding to my last immediate Byrd relative. While I make numerous references to the siblings of direct Byrd kin, there is no attempt to comprehensively document their brothers and sisters.

Any research into the Byrd families of southeast Alabama and their North Carolina heritage should begin with the extensive efforts by Tera Byrd Averett and Charles R. Holloman to compile Byrd genealogical data from public records and individual sources. It would have taken much longer to complete this project without the base of information their work provided.

In an effort to avoid confusion when reading this work, I have taken license to standardize the spelling of my Byrd family line. While evidence clearly shows that this line of Byrds consistently preferred the spelling of their name to contain the letter "y" rather than the letter "i," third parties recording their name in official documents or referring to them in print often interchanged the spelling. Therefore, it took many hours of excruciating research to verify the accounts of some of the ancestors described herein. I am satisfied that, to the best of my ability, the information provided on each direct relative is accurate.

The relatively recent proliferation of ancestry websites on the Internet and the digitization of archived ancestral data from official government sources has revolutionized the accessibility of previously hard-to-obtain records. There is still no substitute for physical presence at ancestral sites, but technology has shortened search time dramatically.

While researching and writing this book, I became aware of a consistent set of traits present in this line of Byrd ancestors. Surprisingly, through ten generations, I have been unable to discover any illegal or unethical behavior on the part of these Byrds. It is possible that I overlooked something along the way, but in my research I made a conscious effort to uncover a juicy story or dark, unscrupulous incident. Certainly, the Byrd line extending from the first William Byrd's nephew—the Westover Byrds, is full of colorful activities regarding the pursuit of wealth, influence, and achievement. But even along this highly scrutinized branch of Byrds, the record is overwhelmingly honorable.

The branch extending directly from the first William

Byrd does not contain a history of accumulated wealth and power, but it is associated with a consistent trail of community participation and devotion to honor, duty, and faith. A letter written by Charles A. Byrd in 1956 and published in Averett, *Byrd History*, p. 237 says it best when describing the previous generation of Byrds in southeast Alabama, "So far as I know, none of these Byrds have ever become great statesmen. They have never aspired to reach political importance. None have accumulated great wealth nor left rich estates. They have been content to live a quiet life and just be the average person in the community where they have lived. Yet, there are at least two characteristics that stand out. In the first place, this generation of Byrds has ever been known as honest people. If they had to make debts, they have paid them on time. Their word has always been their bond. If promises were made, those promises were regarded as sacred trusts.

In the second place, these Byrds are people who have ever been loyal to the Church. From the very beginning, they found their places in the church of their community… For this heritage, we should all be profoundly grateful today."

—Manuel H. Johnson, Jr.

BYRD FAMILY LINE

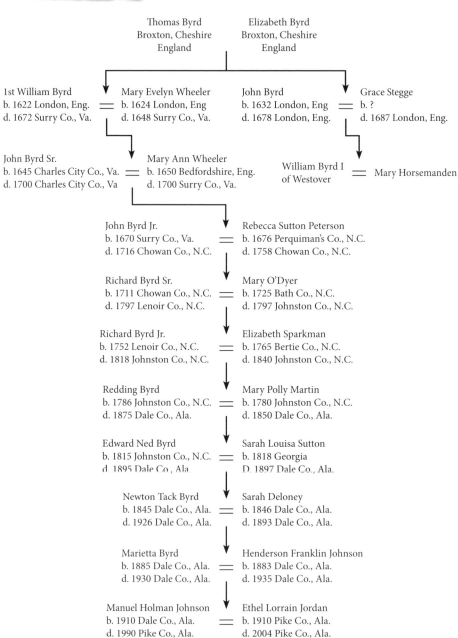

Thomas Byrd
Broxton, Cheshire
England

Elizabeth Byrd
Broxton, Cheshire
England

1st William Byrd
b. 1622 London, Eng.
d. 1672 Surry Co., Va.

Mary Evelyn Wheeler
b. 1624 London, Eng
d. 1648 Surry Co., Va.

John Byrd
b. 1632 London, Eng
d. 1678 London, Eng.

Grace Stegge
b. ?
d. 1687 London, Eng.

John Byrd Sr.
b. 1645 Charles City Co., Va.
d. 1700 Charles City Co., Va

Mary Ann Wheeler
b. 1650 Bedfordshire, Eng.
d. 1700 Surry Co., Va.

William Byrd I
of Westover

Mary Horsemanden

John Byrd Jr.
b. 1670 Surry Co., Va.
d. 1716 Chowan Co., N.C.

Rebecca Sutton Peterson
b. 1676 Perquiman's Co., N.C.
d. 1758 Chowan Co., N.C.

Richard Byrd Sr.
b. 1711 Chowan Co., N.C.
d. 1797 Lenoir Co., N.C.

Mary O'Dyer
b. 1725 Bath Co., N.C.
d. 1797 Johnston Co., N.C.

Richard Byrd Jr.
b. 1752 Lenoir Co., N.C.
d. 1818 Johnston Co., N.C.

Elizabeth Sparkman
b. 1765 Bertie Co., N.C.
d. 1840 Johnston Co., N.C.

Redding Byrd
b. 1786 Johnston Co., N.C.
d. 1875 Dale Co., Ala.

Mary Polly Martin
b. 1780 Johnston Co., N.C.
d. 1850 Dale Co., Ala.

Edward Ned Byrd
b. 1815 Johnston Co., N.C.
d. 1895 Dale Co., Ala.

Sarah Louisa Sutton
b. 1818 Georgia
D. 1897 Dale Co., Ala.

Newton Tack Byrd
b. 1845 Dale Co., Ala.
d. 1926 Dale Co., Ala.

Sarah Deloney
b. 1846 Dale Co., Ala.
d. 1893 Dale Co., Ala.

Marietta Byrd
b. 1885 Dale Co., Ala.
d. 1930 Dale Co., Ala.

Henderson Franklin Johnson
b. 1883 Dale Co., Ala.
d. 1935 Dale Co., Ala.

Manuel Holman Johnson
b. 1910 Dale Co., Ala.
d. 1990 Pike Co., Ala.

Ethel Lorrain Jordan
b. 1910 Pike Co., Ala.
d. 2004 Pike Co., Ala.

CHAPTER I

THE EARLY BYRDS OF VIRGINIA

The name Byrd plays a prominent role in my family history. My grandmother on my father's side was named Marietta Byrd. Also, my great-grandmother, Mary Johnson Byrd, was the adopted stepdaughter of Richard Daniel Byrd, a relative from the same family line. This Byrd line in my father's family goes directly back ten generations to the founders of colonial Virginia.

The first Byrd to arrive in America was William Byrd.[1] Various accounts differ regarding the year that William first arrived on Virginia soil. According to Charles City County records, William sailed to Virginia from England on February 20, 1657 on board the ship *Seven Sisters*, commanded by Captain Abraham Read. However, evidence strongly suggests that William was in Virginia earlier. Although he is clearly recorded on the passenger list, it is likely he was returning from England on business as a mer-

---

1   Stewart, Robert Armistead, "The First William Bird of Charles City County, Virginia," The Virginia Magazine of History and Biography, Vol. 41, No. 3 (July, 1933), pp. 189–195.

chant representative. This seems reasonable since while in England, young William was employed by merchants John Sadler and Thomas Quiney, and became their Virginia representative.[2] In fact, land office patents and grants records in the Library of Virginia show that William Byrd held a patent for 300 acres "upon the south side of Ward's Creek above John Walls dividend" on June 7, 1656.[3]

But the strongest evidence of William Byrd's earlier presence in Virginia is his first marriage to Mary Evelyn Wheeler. Mary was born in London, England in 1624 and likely wed William before the voyage to America, although research by Robert A. Stewart suggests that they were married afterward. Mary and William had a son, John Byrd, reported to be born around 1645 in Southwark Parish, Surry, Virginia. If this is so, William was surely in Virginia at that time. Finally, Mary's death occurred only three years later in 1648 in Southwark Parish, Surry, Virginia almost a

---

2   Charles City County, Virginia, Court Order Book, #1661, p. 564. Also see: "A List of Emigrants from Surviving Records in English Archives," *The Complete Book of Emigrants 1661–1699*, Peter Wilson Coldham, Genealogical Publishing Co., Inc., Baltimore, 1988, p. 71.

3   *Library of Virginia Land Office Patents and Grants*, 1623–1774, Book No. 3, p.249.

decade before William's voyage in 1657.[4]

William was born in London, England about 1622 (some accounts say 1619) to his parents Thomas Byrd and Elizabeth Byrd, a cousin of Thomas'. His father was a silversmith in London. This line of Byrds can be traced back to the Norman Conquest when they first came to England. William had a brother named John, whose son, also named William, immigrated to Virginia later and founded the Westover Byrd dynasty so prominent in colonial history. In addition to his position as Virginia representative for London merchants, William was a local judge and independent businessman.[5]

---

4   Dunlap, D., "William Byrd's Wives," Ancestry.com, posted Dec. 18, 2011; "Mary Evelyn Wheeler Byrd," Ancestry Family Trees; Stewart, "The First William Bird of Charles City County, Virginia," p. 189; Charles City, Virginia Court Order Book, #1661;

Also see US and International Marriage Records, 1560–1900; and Virginia Find a Grave Index, 1607–2012.

5   See Stewart, "The First William Bird of Charles City County, Virginia" p. 190, note, US Find a Grave Index 1600s–current; Virginia, Find a Grave Index, 1607–2012.

Appendix A contains the Byrd family line prepared for William Byrd II of Westover. It documents Byrd family lineage to the Norman Conquest. The Westover Byrds are one of the most, if not the most, documented colonial Virginia families in American history, especially William Byrd II. There are many sources of information on this family.

Just to name a few of the most significant:

William Byrd settled in Martin's Brandon township in Charles City County, Virginia, where he owned and leased many acres. Land transaction records show that he was active in developing his estate most of his adult life. Not long before he died, William purchased a grist mill at the head of Chippokes Creek from a Mr. Thomas Busby along with 450 acres nearby.[6]

Alden Hatch, *The Byrds of Virginia: An American Dynasty, 1670 to the Present* (1969), Holt, Rinehart, and Winston, New York.

The Correspondence of the Three William Byrds of Westover Virginia 1684–1776, Marion Tinling, for the Virginia Historical Society by the University of Virginia Press, Charlottesville, Virginia, 2 Vols., 1977.

The Secret Diary of William Byrd of Westover 1709–1712, Louis B. Wright, The Dietz Press, Inc., Richmond, Virginia, 1941.

William Byrd II, *Histories of the Dividing Line Betwixt Virginia and North Carolina*, Dover Publications, Inc., New York, 1967.

Westover, the plantation of this Byrd family, began as an Indian trading post just over the James River (North side) from the first William Byrd's plantation in Charles City County near Chippokes Creek. The first William Byrd, my direct ancestor, and William Byrd I of Westover's uncle, probably did not know each other well, if at all. William the first died in 1672 and William I of Westover had only been in Virginia a short time before and was still a teenager working for his maternal uncle Thomas Stegge, who actually started the Westover trading post that he inherited.

6 *Library of Virginia Land Office Patents and Grants,* 1623–1774 and Halifax County, Virginia Deed Books 6–8.

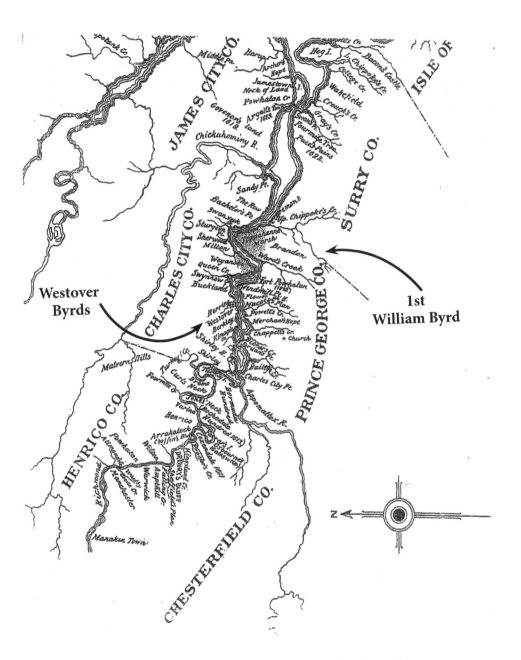

*Colonial James River map showing location of the first William
Byrd at Martin's Brandon and the Byrds of Westover.*

Photo by Flournoy

Westover, the famous early Georgian mansion built by William Byrd II, founder of Richmond, in 1730.

After the death of his first wife, Mary Evelyn Wheeler Byrd, in 1648, William married a second time to Hannah Jennings Grendon, who was the stepsister and sister-in-law of Grace Stegge, the mother of William I of Westover. Hannah and William had two children, Thomas and Elizabeth, both born in Charles City County. Upon William's death in 1672, Thomas inherited his estate. It is not clear why John, William's son by Mary E. Wheeler, was overlooked, but records show that he became the ward of Nevitt Wheeler,

Mary's brother, after Mary's death in 1648. Hannah went on to marry again twice before her death in 1682.[7]

Not much is known about John Byrd except that sometime after his father's death he married Mary Ann Wheeler, his cousin and daughter of Nevitt Wheeler, his uncle and guardian. Interestingly, Nevitt Wheeler was implicated in Nathanial Bacon's Rebellion of 1676, in which colonists protesting the lack of British protection from Indian raids stormed the capital in Jamestown, burned it to the ground, and forced the governor to flee for his life. After Bacon died from disease, the rebellion collapsed and many colonists were hanged for their involvement. Evidently, Nevitt Wheeler escaped the gallows.[8]

---

7   Stewart, Robert Armistead, "The First William Bird of Charles City County, Virginia," p. 190; Coldham, Peter Wilson, *The Complete Book of Emigrants 1661–1699* p. 221.

Mary Evelyn Wheeler was only twenty-four when she died, likely in childbirth. So, her marriage to William was relatively short.

8   Stewart, Robert Armistead, "The First William Bird of Charles City County, Virginia," p. 190.

note: Nevitt Wheeler was not only John Byrd's guardian but seems to have taken responsibility for William Byrd's other children after John Byrd married his daughter Mary Ann Wheeler and William's death in 1672. According to records reported by Stewart, Nevitt became involved in the revolt of 1676, better known as Bacon's Rebellion. Although John Byrd was a married adult by this time, there is no evidence that he was also part of the Rebellion. Historians have presented several theories to explain both the reasons for and impact of Bacon's Rebellion. The most commonly offered cause, mentioned above, is that colonists on the frontier became desperate due to the failure of Virginia Governor Berkeley to deal with murderous Indian raids. Another reason presented is that along with Bacon, other Virginia Council members and planters became fed up with Governor Berkeley favoring his cronies who were getting rich off the Indian trade at the expense of innocent colonists.

It has also been argued that Bacon's Rebellion was driven by class war since those colonists who were landless or indentured servants had no voice. This last argument seems less plausible since the primary leadership of the rebellion came from the planter class. Nevertheless, analysts have reasoned that colonial reforms due to a class-driven revolt, such as phasing out white indentured servitude, began the shift toward reliance on the black slave trade. In the end, Governor Berkely returned and executed twenty-three men by hanging, including the former governor of the Albemarle Sound Colony, William Drummond. Other planters involved but not ring leaders had their land confiscated. This could have happened to Nevitt Wheeler since there are practically no references to him after the Rebellion.

To further understand Bacon's Rebellion and the environment of the time, see the following: Tarter, Brent, "Bacon's Rebellion, the Grievances of the People, and the Political Culture of Seventeenth-Century Virginia," *Virginia Magazine of History and Biography* (2011) 119 #1, pp 1–41;

Wertenbaker, Thomas Jefferson, *Torchbearer of the Revolution: The Story of Bacon's Rebellion and its Leader* (Princeton University Press, 1940);

Washburn, Wilcomb E., *The Governor and the Rebel: A History of Bacon's Rebellion in Virginia* (University of North Carolina Press, 1957);

Billings, Warren M., "The Causes of Bacon's Rebellion: Some Suggestions," *Virginia Magazine of History and Biography*, 1970, Vol. 78, Issue 4, pp. 409–435.

Martin's Brandon Episcopal church and cemetery where the first William Byrd was buried in 1672.

John and Mary Ann appear to have had several children, one of whom was John Byrd, Jr., born around 1670 in Surry County, Virginia. John Jr. has generally been acknowledged as the first Virginia Byrd to migrate to North Carolina. However, there is some evidence that John Sr. may have ventured into North Carolina with his son and then returned to Virginia later. The Colonial Records of North Carolina, Vol. 2 reports that between April and June of 1697, John Byrd petitioned for six "headrights" of land in Albemarle County, North Carolina. For each headright imported into the colony at that time, a person sponsoring the total group could receive, upon application to the court of record, a grant of fifty acres of land. The six persons named in the petition were John Byrd (himself), Mary Byrd (his wife), John Byrd Jr., Mathew Anderson, James Basford, and Richard Wiggins. This would have entitled John Sr. to three hundred acres of land in the county.[9]

These same colonial records also show that John Sr. had a daughter named Hannah Byrd and that in 1684 she was assigned by the local court to live with Mr. Richard Byer until she came of age at twenty-one or first married. This fact would fit with the life of John Byrd Sr. since his stepmother was Hannah Jennings Grendon Byrd. Of course, it is possible that John Sr. filed the headright petition while he was still in Virginia and never moved to Albemarle County, North Carolina since his death occurred only three years later in Surry County, Virginia. After all, it was only about fifty miles to the North Carolina dividing line and just eighty miles to Edenton, the Albemarle County seat. This distance is not far, even by colonial standards.

---

9   Headrights presented to the County Clerk of Albemarle County, Colonial Court Records of North Carolina, miscellaneous papers, #187, 1680–1704. These records were first reported by Charles R. Holloman Sr. in a research paper entitled "The Family Lineage of Mrs. Tera Byrd Averett of Enterprise, Alabama Traced from John Byrd ca. 1675–1716," prepared for Mrs. Tera Byrd Averett and presented in her book, *Byrd History and Related Families of Averett, Calloway, Chancey, and Goff* (Wiregrass Printing Co., 1978), pp. XXI–XLIX.

However, research prepared by Charles R. Holloman, a noted genealogist, indicates that there were three men of the name Byrd or Bird listed in the records of Albemarle County, North Carolina before 1700. Two of these three men were John Byrd and John Byrd Jr.[10]

---

10 The Colonial Records of North Carolina (Second Series) Vol. I (1670–1696) p. 344.

Chapter II

The Byrds of North Carolina

In the late seventeenth and early eighteenth centuries, Albemarle County, North Carolina contained several smaller administrative districts known as precincts. Perquimans Precinct, which later became Perquimans County, was previously named Berkeley in honor of the Governor of Colonial Virginia—the same governor who fled for his life during Bacon's Rebellion. However, settlers kept identifying the area by its Indian name, "Perquimans," and the name was officially changed around 1672. These precincts were included in Anglican church parishes where records were kept. Local courthouses sometimes provided locations for religious services when churches were not yet available. Since the Anglican Church was the recognized state religion in England at this time, there was no attempt to separate church from state.

Church records from this parish in Albemarle County show that John Byrd Jr. and Rebecca Peterson were married on August 24, 1697 by minister John Burnet. Rebecca's original name was Sutton and she was the daughter of

Nathaniel Sutton and his wife Deborah. Rebecca was born August 8, 1676 in Perquimans Precinct. She was first married to Jacob Peterson Jr., who died early in 1697 (month and day unknown). Jacob Peterson Jr. left everything to Rebecca in a statement on his deathbed (a nuncupative will—written down by non-interested witnesses just after death). Also, Jacob's father, Jacob Peterson Sr., left a written will when he died on January 13, 1698 in which he gave "Rebekah Burd, my daughter-in-law" one silver shilling. This will provides clear supporting evidence that Rebecca was married to John Byrd Jr. by this time, since Jacob Sr. referred to her as "Burd."[11]

North Carolina archives indicate that John Byrd Jr. and his wife Rebecca were significant landowners in Perquimans and Chowan Precincts of Albemarle County. These two precincts later became counties in their own right and Albemarle County was officially abolished in 1739. Records

---

11   An abstract entitled "Births, Deaths and Marriages in Berkeley Precinct" from James Robert Bent Hathaway's *The North Carolina Historical and Genealogical Register*, Vol. 3, p. 208, 370, and 373 contains an account of Rebecca Sutton Peterson's parents and her birth in 1676. Also, a summary of Jacob Peterson Sr.'s will can be found in John Bryan Grimes' *Abstracts of North Carolina Wills, 1663–1760* (E.M. Uzzel & Co., 1910), p. 286. A summary from both of these primary sources can be found in Holloman's "The Family Lineage of Tera Byrd Averett," pp. XXIX–XXX.

show that Rebecca sold a large tract of her inherited land to a Mr. Harvey. John Jr. is also listed on the deed of conveyance, but it is clear the land was originally hers since she was represented under power of attorney by Nathaniel Chevin and consented separately to the sale.[12]

John Byrd Jr. at times served as Deputy Marshall and other times as judge of the Admiralty Court of Albemarle County. Admiralty courts were juryless courts located in British colonies and were granted jurisdiction over local legal matters related to maritime activities. In disputes between merchants and seamen, judges were given five percent of any confiscated cargo if they found a smuggling defendant guilty. Also, John Jr. is often referred to as Captain of Militia in the county. Captain of Militia was an important title, both militarily and socially in those days.

John Jr. died in 1716. His will was made on September 13th and probated at the October Court of Common Pleas of Chowan Precinct. In his will, John Bird (Byrd) Jr. left his eldest son John III 640 acres at New Market. His son Edward Byrd was left 365 acres. Son William Byrd inherited 365 acres as well, and youngest son Richard Byrd was

---

12   These land transactions are recorded in Colonial Court Records file #310 of North Carolina Archive vol. 2, p. 33 and also summarized by Holloman in "The Family Lineage of Tera Byrd Averett," pp. XXX–XXXI.

to inherit the home plantation upon the widowhood of wife Rebecca.[13]

Richard Byrd was born in 1711 in Chowan Precinct (county) and came of legal age (21) in 1732. In 1722 when Richard was eleven years old, part of Chowan Precinct (over the Chowan River) was divided into a new precinct called Bertie. Bertie County records show that on May 9, 1732, older brothers John Byrd III and William Byrd authorized their attorney to execute a deed of sale to Richard Byrd. This transfer of land to Richard by his older brothers (possibly acting as guardians) upon his coming of age is consistent with the terms of his father's will, which was probated when he was only five years old.[14]

Although the date is not known exactly, Richard Byrd married Mary Odyer (O'Dyer), daughter of Dennis and Ann Odyer, sometime after 1732 but well before 1741. This time period is likely because in the will of John Stewart,

---

13   An abstracted version of John Byrd Jr.'s will can be found in John Bryan Grimes' *Abstracts of North Carolina Wills*, 1663–1760, p. 59 and is also summarized by Holloman in "The Family Lineage of Tera Byrd Averett," pp. XXXI–XXII.

14   Holloman, "The Family Lineage of Tera Byrd Averett," p. XXXII, summarizes records from the North Carolina Archives, Bertie County Court Minutes for May 9, 1732, pp. 26–27 and Bertie County Deed Book, 1720–1796, E, p. 11.

the son-in-law of Dennis Odyer, written on October 13, 1741 and probated on June 22, 1742, he names John, the young son of Richard Byrd, as an heir of personal property and Richard is named as an executor along with his father-in-law Dennis. Richard is also a witness along with a man named John Herring. Clearly, if John Stewart knew Richard Byrd well enough to name him an executor and witness to his will and include Richard's son as an heir in 1741, the marriage to Mary Odyer must have occurred several years prior. Mary and her parents, the Odyers, lived for some time in the Falling Creek area of Craven Precinct in Bath County, which later became part of newly created Johnston County in 1746. To make matters even more confusing, Craven Precinct was elevated to county status in 1739 and Bath County no longer exists.[15]

Although it is not clear exactly when Richard Byrd arrived in the Falling Creek area of Craven County, records in the North Carolina archives show that he was issued a land grant for 250 acres on November 18, 1739. Evidently, this land lay on the east side of Falling Creek

---

15   Holloman, "The Family Lineage of Tera Byrd Averett," pp. XXXIII–XXXIV. Summarizes court records from Craven and Johnston counties. He also reports material from the North Carolina archives, Secretary of State's office as well as various deed books.

and the north side of the Neuse River. Also, records from the North Carolina State Land Grant Office show that an additional grant of 150 acres was issued to Richard Byrd in the same vicinity of Falling Creek and the Neuse River on March 17, 1740. Over the years from this time, North Carolina colonial records indicate further land grants and land purchases associated with Richard Byrd up until his death in 1797.[16]

By then, Richard Byrd's plantation around Falling Creek had transitioned from Johnston County to Dobbs County and finally to Lenoir County. Richard had become a very prominent figure in this region and served with distinction in his county militia. According to research conducted by Charles R. Holloman, Richard is listed as a commissioned militia officer on a report filed by Colonel Lewis De Rosset, commander of the Johnston County Regiment in the year 1754. This report lists Richard Byrd as lieutenant in company #7.

Later, when Dobbs County was formed in 1759, Richard served as lieutenant in the Dobbs militia. Evidently in

---

16   Holloman, "The Family Lineage of Tera Byrd Averett," p. XXXVII presents land purchase transactions of Richard Byrd Sr. in Craven County. This information is summarized from the North Carolina Archives, "Secretary of State's Papers," file box SS751, and the North Carolina State Land Grant Office Book 5, p. 280 and envelope file #354.

1761, Richard was promoted to Captain of Militia after a tragic accident which killed Charles Young, the previous captain. Holloman explains that Young died at Johnston Courthouse while he slept in his bed in an upstairs room at an inn there after a musket was accidentally fired through the ceiling from the pub below. At this point in his military service, Richard was fifty years old and likely approaching the end of his tenure in the county militia.[17]

From all indications, Richard Byrd and Mary Odyer had three children together. The first child was John Byrd, mentioned earlier. He was born many years before the others, some time prior to 1741 since he is mentioned as an heir in John Stewart's will of that year. Since Mary Odyer's birth date is estimated to be around 1725, some genealogists have speculated that John was the child of a previous marriage of Richard's before he moved to the Falling Creek area. This is unlikely since John Stewart was Dennis Odyer's son-in-law and he would hardly have included young John Byrd as an heir in his will if he were not Mary's natural son. What is more likely is that Mary was very young, perhaps fifteen or sixteen, when John was born. Richard and Mary's second child was Richard Byrd Jr., born in 1752

17   Holloman, "The Family Lineage of Tera Byrd Averett," pp. XXXIX–XL.

and the source of the line of Alabama Byrd ancestors. A third son, Edward, was born about 1762.[18]

By 1780, Richard Byrd Sr. had amassed a large estate in the Falling Creek region of Dobbs County, North Carolina and his sons were starting to find their own way in the community. The 1780 list of taxable estate valuations in Dobbs County shows Richard Byrd Sr.'s taxable estate to be worth 3,092 pounds, a significant sum in those days. Also in 1788, Dobbs County freeholders who voted in the election for constitutional convention representation show both Richard Byrd Sr. and Richard Byrd Jr. on the list. Each voter had to be at least age 21 and own at least fifty acres of land to qualify to be on the list.[19]

During the years after Richard Byrd Sr.'s death in 1797, Richard Jr. appears to have surpassed his father's exten-

18   Edward Byrd is reported as a third son of Richard Byrd Sr. and Mary Odyer by several genealogy websites, sources that are considered reliable since the facts were confirmed by Smart Match. I have been unable to confirm Edward's birth by Mary from primary sources. Mary would have been well into her thirties at the time of Edward's birth, reported as 1762. While certainly possible, Mary's sons would have all been born about ten years apart. The facts are clear regarding Richard Jr.'s birth, and evidence supports the view that youngest son John was born to Mary also.

19   Holloman, "The Family Lineage of Tera Byrd Averett," p. XLIII reports entries from the *Old Grantee Index*, Lenoir County, Vol. 1–21 that show a county list of Dobbs County freeholders in 1780 with their estate valuations.

sive land holdings in the Falling Creek region of what had evolved into Lenoir County, North Carolina. In 1804, Richard Byrd Jr. purchased 4,000 acres of land on Black Creek in Johnston County. Up until his death in 1818, Richard Jr. expanded his estate by an additional 2,500 acres through state land grants so the total land holdings included in his will amounted to at least 6,500 acres.[20]

On July 30, 1785 at the age of thirty-three, Richard Jr. married Elizabeth Sparkman from Bertie County, North Carolina. Elizabeth was twenty years old at the time, born in 1765. Richard Jr. and Elizabeth had eight children together; seven boys and one girl. Two of their sons, Redding and Bright Byrd, became the pioneers that migrated to Alabama in the 1820s and founded the Byrd lineage that rose to prominence in Dale County.[21]

---

20   Richard Byrd Jr.'s will describes landholdings of at least 6,500 acres in the Black Creek area of Johnston County, North Carolina. There are numerous accounts of Richard Jr.'s land transactions in the Johnston County and Lenoir County deed books. Holloman, "The Family Lineage of Tera Byrd Averett," pp. XLVI–XLVIII also summarizes many of these land purchases. Also, a summary of Richard Jr.'s land accumulation is provided on the Rootsweb, Baker family of Harnett County, North Carolina website under [Harnett County Heritage].

21   Richard Byrd Jr. and Elizabeth Sparkman's marriage is listed in the Bertie County, North Carolina Book of Marriage Bonds. The marriage bond was witnessed by George Sparkman.

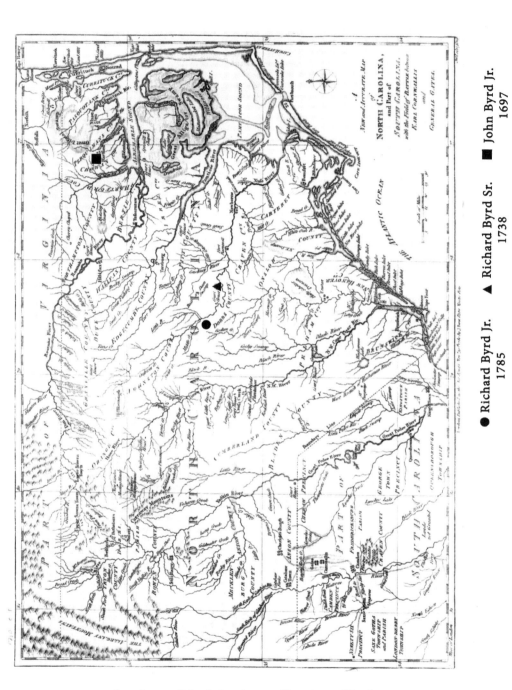

Colonial map of North Carolina and locations of Byrd ancestors.

Like his father, Richard Byrd Jr. served in the North Carolina militia. When the Revolutionary War broke out at Lexington and Concord, Massachusetts on April 19, 1775 followed by Bunker Hill on June 17, 1775, North Carolina colonial governor Josiah Martin proceeded to organize loyalist militia regiments in order to counter patriotic measures to assemble a rebel force.

Richard Jr. sided with the revolutionary patriots and served with the Dobbs County Regiment under Captain Jesse Cobb. He is known to have fought with his regiment against the British loyalist army at the Battle of Moore's Creek Bridge on February 27, 1776.[22] This battle was a pivotal engagement early in the Revolution. British strategists had adopted a divide and conquer plan that involved combining British regular troops with loyalist militia units to divide the colonies and defeat the revolution region by region. Governor Martin's loyalist forces were composed mainly of Scottish highlanders who had migrated to the eastern Carolinas and sworn their allegiance to England after their failed attempt to install a Stuart (Bonnie Prince

---

22   Richard Byrd Jr.'s service in the Revolutionary War and participation in the Battle of Moore's Creek Bridge is documented in the *Revolutionary War Soldier Index for North Carolina and South Carolina*, p. 111 and illustrated in this text.

Charlie) on the English throne in 1745. These troops were commanded by General Donald McDonald, who organized the unit. They proceeded to march toward the coast in order to rendezvous with British regulars commanded by General Sir Henry Clinton, traveling by ship from Boston.

However, the patriot force—including Richard Byrd Jr.—commanded by Colonel James Moore, intercepted the loyalists and blocked their way to the coast. At dawn, the loyalist highlanders attacked the patriots position swinging their broadswords, across a narrow bridge spanning Moore's Creek and were met with blistering musket and cannon fire at point blank range. Within minutes, the loyalist army was in chaotic retreat. In the next few days Colonel Moore's patriot troops captured General McDonald and 850 loyalist soldiers and put an end to Britain's divide and conquer strategy in the South.[23]

---

23   There are many accounts of the Battle at Moore's Creek in 1776. A good summary is provided in Cullen, Joseph P. "Moore's Creek Bridge" *American History Illustrated*, Vol. 4, pp. 10–15, July, 1970.

Revolutionary War Soldiers for NC and SC

State	First	Last	Rank	Unit	Year	Year	Notes	Battles	
							Fall of Charleston, paroled July 1780. Joined Militia and became a Sergeant.	Charleston 1780, Siege of Ninety-Six 1781, Fishing Creek, Kings Mountain, Cowpens.	
SC	John	Byrd	Sergeant				Captured at the Fall of Charleston, paroled in July 1780. At some time, a Sergeant, dates and unit unknown.		
SC	Jonas	Byrd		Hampton's Regiment of Light Dragoons			Served under Capt. John Mills, Lt. Col. Henry Hampton. Dates unknown.		
NC	Joshua	Byrd	Private	Dobbs County Regiment	1776		2/27/1776, a known Private under Capt. Jesse Cobb.	Moore's Creek Bridge.	
NC	Nathan	Byrd	Drummer	Dobbs County Regiment	1776		2/27/1776, a known Drummer under Capt. Jesse Cobb.	Moore's Creek Bridge.	
SC	Reiden	Byrd			1781	1782	330 Days in Militia 1781-1782. Unit unknown.		
NC	Richard	Byrd	Private	Dobbs County Regiment	1776		2/27/1776, a known Private under Capt. Jesse Cobb.	Moore's Creek Bridge.	
NC	Robert	Byrd		Dobbs County Regiment	1777		7/26/1777, drafted under Capt. John Kennedy.		
NC	Robert	Byrd	Private	Duplin County Regiment	1776		2/27/1776, a known Private under Capt. Michael King.	Moore's Creek Bridge.	
NC	Thomas	Byrd		Dobbs County Regiment	1777		7/26/1777, drafted under Capt. John Kennedy.		

Revolutionary War Soldier Index for NC and SC

Revolutionary War Soldier Index showing Richard Byrd Jr.'s service in the war.

Site of the Battle of Moore's Creek Bridge, North Carolina.

It is not clear how long Richard Jr. served in the Revolution or how many other engagements he fought. Colonial records contain a Revolutionary War-era pay voucher to Richard Byrd as late as April 7, 1783, well after the fall of Yorktown on October 19, 1781. Of course, many patriot soldiers went unpaid for long periods of time before resolving their claims. However, many military units remained in service because British troops were not withdrawn until 1783.[24]

One of the best preserved early documents in North Carolina is the last will and testament of Richard Byrd Jr. dated November 12, 1807. This will was drafted in long-hand by Richard Jr.'s legal representative and properly witnessed. Upon Richard Jr.'s death in 1818, the will was filed and probated in the November court of that year. In his will, Richard Jr. left his surviving children equal parcels of his landholdings. Each of his sons and daughter were left 638 acres of land. While not written in Richard Jr.'s will, his wife Elizabeth was entitled by North Carolina law at the time to one-third of the estate unless otherwise specified.

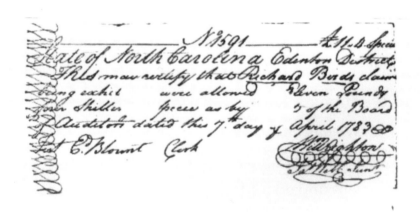

Revolutionary War pay voucher for Richard Byrd Jr.

---

24   See the pay voucher to Richard Byrd Jr. (Bird) illustrated in this text.

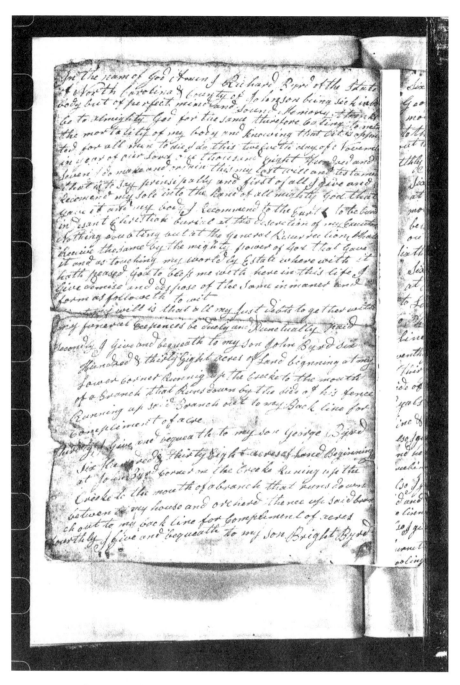

Well-preserved hand-written will of Richard Byrd Jr., dated 1807.

Six Hundred & thirty Eight acres of Land begining at
George Byrd Corner Joining up the Creeke to the
mouth of the mill branch thence up said branch
to the mouth of the mide branch thence up said branch
out to my back line for compliment of acres

thly I give and bequeal to my Son Richard Byrd
Six Hundred & thirty Eight acres of Land Begining
at Bright Byrd Corner thence up the Creeke to the
mouth of a little Branch that runs in to the Creeke
below the mouth of the medow branch thence
out to the big Branch for Compliment of acres

Sixthly I give and bequeath to my son Redin Byrd
Six Hundred & thirty Eight acres of Land begining
at Richard Byrd Corner Thence up the Creeke
to Coz Mathies line thence along said Mathews
to Philip Johnston line thence along said Johnson
line Large Enough to git his Compliment of acres
venthly to my Daughter Elizabeth Allin Six Hundred
thirty Eight acres of land & two hundred on the other
ide of mingo Joining of Samuel Cox line and Bruton
yats line the rest of it between Philip Johnston
line & Redin Byrds line to make up his Compliment of acres
eso I give to my son Georg Byrd one mare and feathe plow
ne nearwst one feather bed and furniture one Cow & one
sucking hoe
lso I give to my Daughter Elizabeth Allin one feather
d and furniture one flat byron one wooling wheel &
e linning wheel
eso I give to my son Bright Byrd one feather bead and
urniture one Cow and Calf I want Bright to have two years
ooling and the Rent of his plentation to pay for it

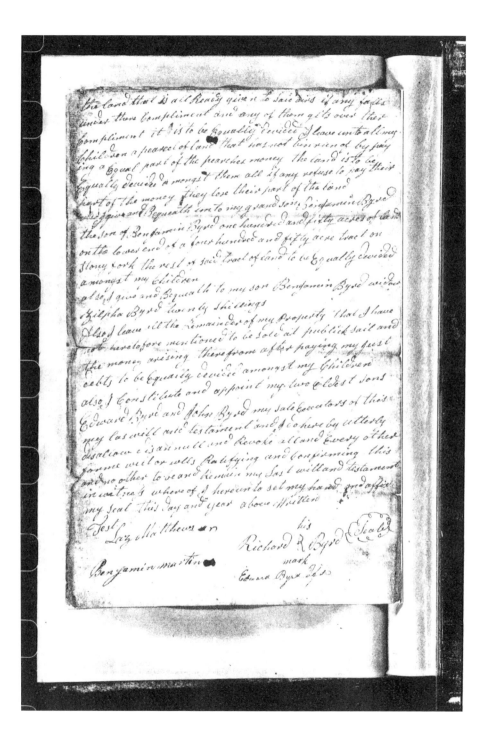

the land that is all Ready given to said diss if any fails
under there Compliment and any of them gits over there
Compliment it is to be Equally devided I leave unto all my
Children a pearcel of land that has not been revewd by paying a Equal part of the pearches money the land is to be
Equally devided amongst them all if any refuse to pay their
part of the money they lose their part of the land
I give and Bequeath unto to my grand son Benjamin Byrd
the son of Benjamin Byrd one hundred and fifty acres of land
on the lower end of a four hundred and fifty acre tract on
Stony cork the rest of said tract of land to be Equally devided
amongst my Children
also I give and Bequeath to my son Benjamin Byrd widow
Zilpha Byrd twenty shillings
Also I leave all the remainder of my Property that I have
not heretofore mentioned to be sold at publick sail and
the money arising therefrom after paying my just
debts to be Equally devided amongst my Children
also I Constitute and appoint my two oldest sons
Edward Byrd and John Byrd my sole Executors of this
my las will and testament and I do hereby utterly
disallow disanull and Revoke all and Every other
former will or wills Ratifying and Confirming this
and no other to be and hemein my last will and testament
in witness whereof I hereunto set my hand and affix
my seal this day and year above Written

Test Lazs Mathews

Benjamin martin

Richard R Byrd {Seal}
his
mark

Edward Byrd Jur

Richard Jr. also provided for the wife of his deceased son Benjamin and their child. His remaining assets were to be sold and the proceeds equally distributed to the children.[25] At the time Richard Jr.'s will was probated, Redding Byrd was thirty-two years old and Bright Byrd was twenty-eight. These two brothers would remain in Johnston County, North Carolina for another decade before deciding to move their families to Alabama.

In 1806, when he was twenty years old, Redding married Mary Polly Martin. Records indicate that Mary was born about 1780 and therefore was older than Redding. Redding and Mary proceeded to raise a large family of eleven children. Ten of these children were born in North Carolina before the move to Alabama.[26]

---

25   See the well-preserved original of Richard Byrd Jr.'s will illustrated in this text. Also, early American regulations on wills and testaments in North Carolina can be found in the section on "Wills, Intestates, and Probates," Bob's Genealogy Filing Cabinet: Southern and Colonial Genealogies.

26   Not much is known about Mary Polly Martin. All references to her are associated with the records of her husband, Redding Byrd, and her children. Her marriage to Redding is reported in Averett, Tera Byrd, *Byrd History*, p. 92. Several sources on family ancestry websites document her marriage to Redding Byrd and report the date as 1806. One such site is www.adkins9.net. In reading extensively through material on Byrd family history, it appears obvious that the Byrd and Martin families were intertwined socially and geographically in both North Carolina and Alabama.

For twenty-two years, Redding and Mary built their estate in Johnston County. It appears that they were relatively prosperous, especially after Richard Jr. willed a significant piece of his land to Redding in 1818. There are some land records that document other purchases by Redding in 1814. Also as early as 1807, Redding posted a marriage bond for his sister Elizabeth (Betsy) and Demsey Allen in the amount of 500 pounds. This was a considerable pledge from a young man, given that North Carolina prohibited state-produced currency at the time and private notes stated in pounds were often backed by precious metal.[27]

Unfortunately, economic prospects in North Carolina began to change considerably in the early nineteenth century. A deteriorating economy and the promise of great new opportunities on the US frontier led to a huge wave of out migration. North Carolina possessed the third largest population in the country in 1790, but by 1860 the state

---

Mary Polly Martin's name has been passed down to numerous relatives over the years since her life with Redding, even though there is very little official documentation of her existence.

27   Several land transactions by Redding Byrd in North Carolina are recorded in North Carolina Archives, *Abstracts of Johnston County Record of Estates*, Vol. VIII. A photocopy of the actual marriage bond document signed by Redding Byrd is shown in Averett, *Byrd History*, p. 270 and is easily accessed when searching Redding Byrd on most ancestry search sites.

had fallen to twelfth in rank. Also by 1860, thirty percent of North Carolina's native-born population was living in some other state or territory.[28]

Several reasons have been offered to explain the decline of the North Carolina economy in the early 1800s. Probably the most prominent argument was weakening soil productivity resulting from a lack of crop rotation. Farmers in the region simply grew the same crops every year until the soil was spent and then moved on to new, uncultivated areas. Many proponents of progressive government blamed this trend on poor educational opportunities and a lack of public commitment to infrastructure development. While there is probably some truth to this argument, it is more likely that cheap land availability from government grants to attract new settlement caused low value to be assigned to property (almost like common property) and therefore little incentive to invest in productive land use methods.[29]

Also, in North Carolina during the colonial period,

28   See Lennon, Donald R., and Ragan, Fred D. "Searching for Greener Pastures: Outmigration in the 1800s and 1900s," *Tar Heel Junior Historian* 34, no. 2 (Spring 1995) North Carolina Museum of History.

29   A good overview of agricultural production in the post-Revolutionary War period of the South can be found in *The South in the Building of the Nation* (1909). The Southern Historical Publication Society, Richmond, Virginia, Vol. 5, Economic History, 1607–1865, pp. 152–168.

tobacco and the warehouse receipts backed by stored tobacco were accepted as currency. As you might expect, if you could grow your own currency, too much would be produced and the value would decline.[30] So, the low price of agricultural production simply meant there was little reason to invest heavily to further increase the supply of commodities already excessively available. If the market price of agricultural production had been favorable enough to generate significant profit, plantation owners and small farmers would have pushed for better roads and port facilities. And later, as cotton prices moved up throughout the South due to global demand, North Carolina began to pursue better means of processing and delivering cotton to the market.[31] The availability of cheap land and slave labor, however, continued to suppress the use of crop rotation strategies.

---

30   See, for example, Johnson, Manuel H., "Tobacco as Money in Colonial Virginia and Carolina," Florida State University, Graduate Research Studies in Monetary Theory and Policy, 1976.

Also see Ferguson, E.J. "Currency Finance: An Interpretation of Colonial Monetary Practices" *William and Mary Quarterly,* April 1953, 10, pp. 153–180.

31   A good presentation of agricultural developments in North Carolina and the South in general and the impact on industrial innovation and transportation infrastructure is provided in *The South in the Building of the Nation,* Vol. 5, pp 152–274 and pp. 313–380.

While the economy of North Carolina was mired in depression in the early 1800s, new US territories were opening up in the deep south and west. Hostile Creek Indian factions in Alabama territory had been defeated by US volunteer forces commanded by General Andrew Jackson in 1814, culminating with his victory at the Battle of Horseshoe Bend on March 27th.[32] By 1819, Alabama territory had achieved statehood. US treaties with the Creek tribes still governed much of the land use in parts of the new state, including the southeastern area. While ultimate removal of the Creeks and other southern tribes became inevitable, initially many Indians were allowed to remain on some of their traditional lands, especially in the eastern part of Alabama. Attempts by the federal government to enforce these treaties caused serious friction with Alabama officials and speculative settlers that were flocking to the area to lay claims on the best land.[33]

---

32   A brief discussion of the Battle of Horseshoe Bend can be found in Rogers, William Warren: Ward, Robert David; Atkins, Leah Rawls; and Flynt, Wayne, *Alabama; The History of a Deep South State* (1994) University of Alabama Press, pp. 52–53. For a thorough reading on Horseshoe Bend and the Creek Wars, see *Remini*, Robert V. *Andrew Jackson and his Indian Wars* (2001) Viking Penguin and Pickett, Albert James *History of Alabama* (1851) Walker and James Publishing, Charleston, Vol. II.

33   For an examination of the difficulties in resolving the treaties

In the 1830 US Census, the population of Alabama was counted as 309,527, a 142 percent increase over 1820. In a recent Alabama history book by Rogers, Ward, Atkins, and Flynt, the authors quote a letter written by James Graham of Lincoln County, North Carolina in which he states, "The Alabama fever rages here with great violence and has carried off vast numbers of our citizens."[34] These same authors point out that "In the older Southern States, plantation families whose profits were being reduced by worn-out lands, encouraged younger sons to seek their fortunes and financed the move with slaves, farm animals, and supplies."[35]

---

with the Creek tribes and associated settlement and political issues, see McCorvey, Thomas Chalmers, *Alabama Historical Sketches* (1960) The University Press of Virginia, Charlottesville, chapter 2, pp 33–64.

34 Rogers, Ward, Atkins, and Flynt, *Alabama: The History of a Deep South State*, p. 54.

35 Rogers, Ward, Atkins, and Flynt, *Alabama: The History of a Deep South State*, p. 55.

CHAPTER III

THE BYRDS OF ALABAMA

In an account written by W.L. Andrews in 1899, Redding Byrd and his family, along with other settlers, departed their homes in North Carolina headed for the wiregrass area of Alabama on February 20, 1828. When the earliest pioneers came to this region, they were very impressed by the vast open meadows of head-high grasses that appeared as waves. The journey took exactly one month traveling in wagons and horse carts. They probably followed the old Federal Road toward Montgomery until it branched southward on Three Notch Road or the Improved Road of 1819 which entered directly into Dale County. All of these roads were really trails in poor condition and could hardly sustain a wagon train without a considerable struggle. Also, they were heavily worn from continuous streams of migrant families seeking their fortunes. Redding was accompanied by William Martin, who was appointed leader of the expedition since it was his second trip. Additionally, William was likely related to Mary Polly Martin Byrd. Accounts of the trip mention that a contingent of

Johnsons were also among the group.[36]

Upon entering Alabama, Redding Byrd camped at the farm of William Andrews located about two miles southeast of the area that eventually became the settlement called Ozark. After a stay on the Andrews' farm for two weeks, Redding and his family moved to an area one mile east of Ozark, which became known as Carroll Church after Redding sold this land to Reuben Carroll and friends built a Primitive Baptist building on the site. Eventually, Redding settled his family across the Claybank Creek, west of Ozark in an area that was to become part of Fort Rucker military reservation which is now the US Army helicopter training facility.[37]

---

36   The account of Redding Byrd's migration with his family to Dale County is published in Andrews, W.L. "Early History of Southeast Alabama," serial article, Southern Star Publishing, Ozark, Alabama, May 17, 1899. This article is also presented in Averett, *Byrd History*, pp. 346–349. A good explanation of the road/trail conditions is found in Rogers, Ward, Atkins, and Flynt, *Alabama: The History of a Deep South State*, pp. 55–57. Mention of a contingent of Johnsons traveling with Redding Byrd and his family is found in the research article Keller, SP5 Meredith, "Ft. Rucker Cemeteries: Echoes of the Past," The Army Flier publication, February 13, 1975, p. 10.

37   Redding Byrd's move from the Carroll Church area to Claybank Creek is documented in the article, "The Sing at Carroll Church," Southern Star Publishing, Ozark, Alabama, May, 1904. Also, see Andrews, W.L., "Early History of Southeast Alabama," June 28, 1899.

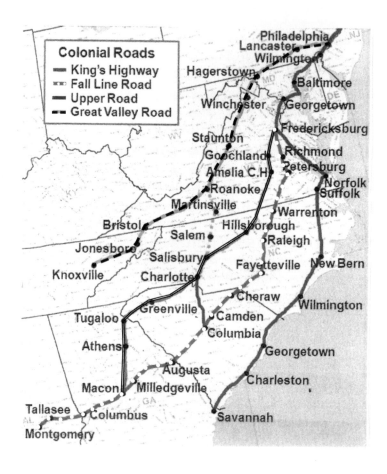

Pioneer roads used by early settlers. Redding Byrd's family likely traveled the Fall Line (Federal) Road into Alabama.

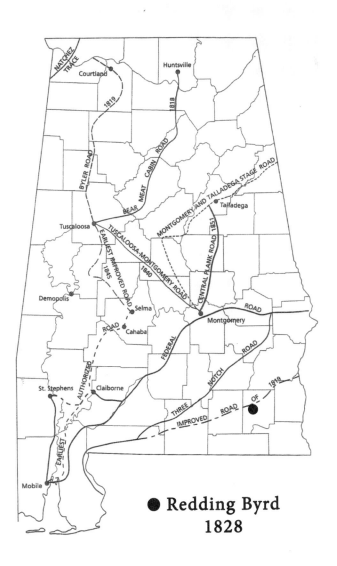

Early Roads in Alabama

Upon entering Alabama, Redding Byrd and family would have followed the Federal Road to the Three Notch or Improved Road of 1819.

Redding Byrd and Mary Polly Martin Byrd spent the rest of their lives in this area of Dale County. Many of Redding and Mary's children, especially the older ones, also made their homes in this part of Dale County. The other surviving children migrated to Arkansas. There are several land transactions by Redding recorded in the federal Homestead and Cash Entry Patent archives that indicate fairly significant land holdings in this area of Alabama.[38]

Much of the social life of Alabama pioneer families centered around churches they established as places of worship and meetings. Redding and his sons Isaac, Curtis, and William helped establish Claybank Church in 1829 when the family moved into the vicinity. According to research conducted by Emmie Martin Hunt, "the site selected was centrally located for the settlers, about one-half mile from Claybank Creek and one and one-half mile from the present town of Ozark. This was, at that time public land, and was part of a large scope of uncut wood-

---

38   At least two land grant transactions are attributed to Redding Byrd in United States, Bureau of Land Management, Mississippi, Homestead, and Cash Entry patents, pre-1908. Mississippi includes Alabama territory covered under Indian treaties. On November 10, 1840 Redding purchased forty acres and on April 2, 1850 he purchased 318 acres. This second purchase seems very late in his life, however, most accounts of Redding's death are around 1875. There are obviously earlier homestead grants from his initial settlement.

land… a settlement road passed along the south side of the church, and an old Indian trail on the east side."[39]

Claybank Church was originally nondenominational, but by 1831 had become affiliated with Methodists. Since Redding was a Primitive Baptist, he eventually moved his affiliation to Darian Church, where he worshiped for the rest of his life and was buried there with Mary Polly Martin Byrd. Darian Church no longer exits and its cemetery was absorbed into Fort Rucker military reservation in the 1940s. The graves that were clearly marked were moved to Pleasant Hill Methodist Church Cemetery. However, by this time Redding and Mary Polly Martin's headstones had disappeared and so their graves remain on the old church site inside Fort Rucker.[40]

---

39   See Hunt, Emmie Martin, "Old Claybank Church," *Alabama Historical Quarterly*, Vol. 1, no. 4 Winter issue, 1930.

40   Murray, Jan Lee "Fort Rucker History: Many Cemeteries Moved in 1942," jmurray@southeastsun.com, March 23, 2016. There are many other family history accounts of ancestors' gravesites moved or lost in the development of Fort Rucker. Redding Byrd and Mary Polly Martin Byrd are mentioned in several of these oral history records. For example, Adkins Family Genealogy, History & Heritage, www.adkins.ws/individual.php?pid=17001.

Possibly, one of the reasons Redding and Bright Byrd left North Carolina for Alabama was the split between the traditional Baptist Church and the Primitive Baptist movement, an "old school" New Testament view that

Claybank Church. Byrd family members helped build the original structure in the early 1800s.

Believed to be an image of Redding Byrd or oldest son Isaac in the late 1850s or early 1860s.

objected to the Baptist Church trend toward mission boards and temperance societies.

The sixth child of Redding and Mary Polly Martin was Edward (Ned) Byrd, my great-great-grandfather. Ned was born on June 22, 1815 in Johnston County, North Carolina. He was fourteen years old when the family moved to Dale County, Alabama in 1828. Ned appears to have been an industrious young man who was active in the community around Claybank and Ozark. In 1839 he married Sarah Louisa Sutton, who had been born in Georgia in 1818. Together they raised a family of eight children; five boys and three girls. Ned and Louisa (preferred name) were active in Darian Primitive Baptist Church and Ned was also involved as a freemason in the Claybank area Masonic organization.[41]

Federal land records indicate that Ned Byrd became a fairly significant landholder and farmer around the Claybank area of Ozark. There are numerous listings of land transactions by Edward Byrd in the Homestead and Cash Entry Patent archives as well as the Index of Federal Land Grants. Again, this area was mostly absorbed into the Fort Rucker military reservation in the 1940s.

---

41   See Averett, Tera Byrd, *Byrd History* pp. 92, 150–157. Also see US Census, 1860, Newton District. Edward Ned Byrd and his entire family are listed on this document. Ned Byrd's gravestone illustrated in this text contains a masonic logo at the top of the marker and his obituary in the local news paper describes a masonic ceremony.

Edward 'Ned' Byrd and Sarah Louisa Sutton Byrd in the 1870s.

By most accounts, Ned's father, Redding Byrd, died in 1875 at the age of eighty-nine.[42] So, Ned built his estate without the assistance of an inheritance. Data from the

---

42 There are at least nine land transactions by Edward Byrd listed in Alabama, Homestead and Cash Entry Patents, Pre-1908. Dates of these records range from December 1, 1851 to November 1, 1858 and amount to about 680 acres.

Most accounts of Redding Byrd's death indicate a date of 1875 at the age of 89. However, some accounts simply say after 1850 since Redding is not listed in the US Census as head of household after that time. It is possible that since Mary Polly Martin Byrd died in 1850, Redding sold or transferred his farm and lived with other family members up until 1875.

1860 US Census when Ned was forty-five years old show that he had by that time compiled an estate valued at $4,200.[43] This was a considerable sum in those days. In 2016 dollars, his assets would be worth about $10 million if compounded at a five percent annual rate.

Unfortunately, Ned and Louisa Byrd's family was about to experience the most horrific cataclysm in United States history. When historians write about families and the fabric of society being torn apart by the American Civil War, they could have been directly referring to the Alabama Byrds of Dale County and the wiregrass area. Mostly, the sons of Ned Byrd's generation became the soldiers of the Confederate States army and the daughters became the widows. Ned and Louisa lost both their two oldest sons to the war and saw another son wounded, captured, and imprisoned. Ned's brothers' families fared no better. His older brother Curtis also lost his oldest son and saw another wounded. By the 1870 US Census, five years after the end of the war, only youngest son Isaac (ten years old) and daughters with few male prospects remained in the household.[44]

---

43 Regarding the value of Ned Byrd's estate, see US Census, 1860, Newton District, Edward Bird, no. 740.

44 In the National Archives, Index to Compiled Service Records of Confederate Soldiers, compiled 1903–1927, documenting period 1861–

The value of Ned's real estate assets had declined by thirty percent, even in US (not Confederate) dollar terms. There is no evidence that Ned owned slaves before or during the war. His farm was likely tended by his large family before the war, went mostly dormant during the conflict, and was scaled back with hired cheap labor or share-cropped after the war. Ned and Louisa lived on until the mid-1890s, loyal to their community and church, and able to enjoy watching their remaining children and grandchildren progress.

My great-grandfather Newton Tack Byrd was born on September 17, 1845 and was the third son of Ned and Louisa. He was the first Byrd in my direct line to be born in Alabama. As far as I can tell, he was referred to as "Tack" all his life. It is not clear what originated this nickname, but it stuck to him (no pun intended).

1865, Pub. M311, N A Catalog ID 586957, Record Group 109, there is an original letter from Edward Ned Byrd to Confederate and Alabama state authorities dated August 19, 1863, informing them of the death of their son, Charles B. Byrd of Co. I, 33rd Alabama Infantry Regiment, on June 18, 1863, while at home suffering from war wounds. Records from the same National Archives Index show that Ned's brother Curtis lost his son Benjamin G. Byrd as a result of severe dysentery contracted while serving with the same unit in 1862. Also, Curtis Byrd's son, Daniel M. Byrd was discharged from the 33rd Alabama after wounds that were complicated by severe bronchitis. Finally, Ned's thinned family is reported in the US Census, 1870, Newton District, Edward Byrd, no. 31.

Gravestones of Edward Ned Byrd and Louisa Sutton Byrd. These graves were moved to Pleasant Hill Cemetery from Darian Cemetery when Fort Rucker expanded in the 1940s.

Tack had hardly matured out of childhood when political tensions between northern and southern states began to heat up and boil over. The 1860 US Census reports Newton Tack Byrd as fifteen years old, so the information would have been obtained after September. Tack's two older brothers Charles B. and Curtis W. were listed as twenty and eighteen years old respectively, already old enough to legally enlist as soldiers.[45]

---

45   See the US Census, 1860, Newton District, Edward Byrd, no. 740.

On November 6, 1860, Abraham Lincoln of the Republican Party was elected President of the United States. Although Lincoln's position was balanced and he personally supported the protection of southern states' rights, including slave holding, he opposed the expansion of slavery into new US territory. Southern politicians considered the new territory question on slavery to be critical since without future state self-determination, US expansion automatically meant that abolitionists' views would ultimately control the federal government and the South would be forced to change its way of life.[46]

By December 17, 1860, South Carolina had seceded from the United States. On January 11, 1861, Alabama became the fourth state to secede. Events moved so fast from this point that by February a new government was being formed in Montgomery and on April 12th, war broke out when Fort Sumter, a United States property in Charleston Harbor, South Carolina, was fired on by Confederate States forces. On May 20th the Confederate Congress voted to move the capitol to Richmond, Virginia after the state

---

46   For a more detailed explanation of Abraham Lincoln's policy views and southern political dynamics after the 1860 presidential election see Goodwin, Doris Kearns, *Team of Rivals*, (2005) Simon & Schuster, New York, pp. 293–295.

decided to secede. Everywhere in the South, local militia units were forming and gradually converting to regular army regiments as they organized at various central locations.[47]

The first regular army regiment to organize in Alabama was the First Alabama Infantry Regiment. Companies were enlisted by recruiting officers from various parts of the state. Initially, most companies were enlisted for one year since no one expected the war to become a five-year nightmare. The First Alabama had the distinction of being the first unit to enlist for one year, the first to reenlist (this time for three years), and to survive from the beginning to the very end of the conflict. All of the companies of the First were actually assembled together for the first time in Pensacola, Florida, where they were trained and assigned to harbor defense. The Regiment was reenlisted for three years in early 1862 and moved to the Mississippi River theatre at Island No. 10 where Tennessee, Kentucky, and Missouri intersect.[48]

---

47   For a day-to-day summary of major events during the period 1861–1865 see Long, E.B., *The Civil War Day by Day* (1971) Da Capo Press, New York.

48   For a history of the 1st Alabama Infantry Regiment, see Wheeler, Lieutenant General Joseph, *Confederate Military History: Alabama* (1899) Vol VII, Part I, Chap. IV, pp. 52–56.

One of the first soldiers to sign up with the First Alabama for the new three-year enlistments was John R. Johnson, my great-great-grandfather. His company muster role shows that he enlisted February 17, 1862 at Perote, Alabama. He was thirty-four years old at the time and had a wife named Sarah Whittington Johnson, age thirty-one, and a new daughter named Mary, age two.[49] Four months earlier, anticipating his enlistment, John R. visited with his friend Richard Daniel Byrd, Newton Tack Byrd's cousin, and asked him to look after his wife and child if anything happened to him.[50] On October 7, 1861 Richard enlisted for three years with Company I of the Fifteenth Alabama

---

49   John R. Johnson's Muster Roll card with the 1st Alabama Infantry Regiment, Co. I is illustrated in this text and can be found in the National Archives, Index to Compiled Service Records of Confederate Soldiers.

The US Census, 1860, Dale County, Alabama, Newton District, p. 119, no. 812 shows John R. Johnson, his wife Sarah, and daughter Mary. His assets at this time were valued at $540. All three family members were reported to be born in North Carolina, including Mary, who was only one year old. So, John R. Johnson and Sarah Whittington Johnson were recent arrivals to Alabama.

50   The story about the relationship between Richard Daniel Byrd and John R. Johnson handed down through Richard's family is found in Averett, *Byrd History,* p. 465. This friendship would have been relatively new since John R. Johnson and his family had only been in Dale County for slightly over a year. This is not surprising, since John had no close relatives nearby to confide in at the time.

Infantry Regiment and was shipped off to Virginia where the unit was already encamped near Centreville around the Manassas battleground where the first large conflict of the war was fought.[51]

Tack Byrd was only sixteen years old and under age when the war broke out in 1861. However, his oldest brother Charles B. Byrd and eight of his Byrd cousins all enlisted in the 33rd Alabama Infantry Regiment. Cousins Benjamin G., Curtis, Daniel M., Elisha Edward, Ransom, Steven C., and William B. all signed up with Company I at Ozark on March 4, 1862. Brother Charles B. and cousin W.C. Byrd enlisted in Company I at Montgomery on May 9, 1862.[52]

---

51   Richard Daniel Byrd's Muster Roll card with the 15th Alabama Infantry Regiment, Co. E is illustrated in this text and can be found in the National Archives, Index to Compiled Service Records of Confederate Soldiers.

52   The entire roster of Company I, 33rd Alabama Infantry Regiment is listed in History of the 33rd Alabama, www.33rdalabama.org/companyi. htm. Also see a summary of the 33rd Alabama in Wheeler, Lieutenant General Joseph E., *Confederate Military History*, pp. 160–164.

Company muster roll for John R. Johnson of the First Alabama Infantry Regiment during the Civil War.

Page No. 119

617

SCHEDULE 1.—Free Inhabitants in _____ in the County of Dale State of Alabama enumerated by me, on the 11th day of Aug 1860. Wm Brownell Ass't Marshal.

Post Office Newton

		The name of every person whose usual place of abode on the first day of June, 1860, was in this family.	Age	Sex	Color	Profession, Occupation, or Trade	Value of Real Estate	Value of Personal Estate	Place of Birth				
		Mary A	25	F					Ga				
		Joseph G	12	M					"				
		Daniel T	11						"				
		Wm A	10						"			/	
		James Thomas	10						"			/	
		Clancy	8	F					"			/	
		Julia A	7	"					"			/	
		Neiry W	1	M					Ala				
		Hezekiah Dean	79	F					Md				
		Martha	42	"					Ga				
		Samuel	15	"					"				
809	809	Hester Mixon	34	M		Farmer	730	755	S.C				
		Mary A G	20	F					Ga				
		Jane E	3	"					Ala				
		George T	2	M					"				
		Sarah J	4/12	F					"				
810	810	James Elmore	27	M				250	S.C			/	
		Sarah J	27	F					"				
		William V	5	M					"				
		Mary J	1	F					Ala				
811	811	Edward Stephens	45	M			2500	1188	N.C			/	
		Mary	38	F					Ala			/	
		Nancy	7						"				
		Mary	4						"				
		Wm J	1	M					"				
812	812	John R Johnson	33				240	300	N.C				
		Sarah	30	F					"				
		Mary	1						"				
813	813	John Loyd	52	M			1377	150	"			/	
		Sarah	30	F					S.C			/	
		Henry	16	M		Farm Laborer			N.C			/	
		Archy A	5						Ala				
		Sarah	3	F					"				
		Lency A	9/12						"				
		James Foxworth	26	M				75	"				
		Jane C	17	F					Ga				
		Amanda E	2						Ala				
		Sarah J C	3/12						"				
814	814	Barry Barby	30	M				100	"				
		Rosa	21	F					"			/	

No. white males, 47. No. colored males, ____. No. foreign born, ____. No. blind, ____. No. idiotic, ____. No. convicts, ____.
No. white females, 48. No. colored females, ____. No. deaf and dumb, ____. No. insane, ____. No. paupers, ____. 3,610 | 2,798

The 1860 US Census showing John R. Johnson, wife Sarah Whittington Johnson, and one-year-old child Mary Johnson.

Tragedy with the Byrd family and friends came quickly once these young men were exposed to combat. Six of the nine Byrd relatives that joined the 33rd Alabama were either dead or wounded by 1864. Tack's older brother Charles B. was wounded in June of 1863 and sent home where he died on June 18th. Although Ned and Louisa, Tack's parents, were still grieving over Charles' death, Tack in response went out and enlisted in Company I of the 33rd Alabama on July 1st, just two weeks after Charles' death. Quite often in an emotional reaction, young men enlisted in the war after a close relative or friend's tragic death.[53]

After enlisting with the 1st Alabama in February, John R. Johnson's regiment was deployed to Memphis, Tennessee in March of 1862. From Memphis, the regiment was moved to Island No. 10, which was a fort positioned inside a sharp turn of the Mississippi River. This fort was a key position that made it very difficult to use ships for transporting Union troops and supplies down the river. Its vulnerability was that it could be isolated and cut off if Union forces seized the Tennessee side of the river where Con-

---

53   Newton Tack Byrd's Muster Roll card with the 33rd Alabama Infantry Regiment, Co. I is illustrated in this text and can be found in the National Archives, Index to Compiled Service Records of Confederate Soldiers.

federate troops supplied and protected the fort. Eventually, Union engineers dug a canal that bypassed Island No. 10 and allowed transport boats to ferry troops across the river to the south of the island, blocking a retreat and escape. A few Confederate troops, including some of the 1st Alabama, managed to escape, but the vast majority were forced to surrender on April 8th.[54]

John R. Johnson was sent to prison at Camp Douglas in Chicago, Illinois. This camp became notorious for its severe conditions and hostile treatment of prisoners. John R. died there just before a prisoner exchange could be arranged in September, 1862. He is buried in a mass grave containing 6,000 Confederate prisoners who died there between 1862–1865. His name and unit are engraved on one of the metal plates on the monument.[55]

---

54   For a thorough account of actions involving the 1st Alabama at Island Number 10 see *Battles and Leaders of the Civil War* (1887) The Century Co., DeVinne Press, New York, Vol. I, pp. 430–452, pp. 460–463.

55   John R. Johnson's prisoner of war death report can be found in the National Archives, Register of Confederate Soldiers, Sailors, and Citizens Who Died in Federal Prisons and Military Hospitals in the North, 1861–1865, M918. For a thorough study of Camp Douglas, Illinois see Levy, George, *To Die in Chicago: Confederate Prisoners at Camp Douglas 1862–1865* (1994) Pelican Publishing, Gretna Louisiana. Also see Pucci, Kelley, *Camp Douglas: Chicago's Civil War Prison*, (2007) Arcadia Publishing.

Mass grave and memorial in Chicago dedicated to Confederate soldiers who died at Camp Douglas POW compound during the Civil War. John R. Johnson is buried here and listed on the memorial.

Richard Daniel Byrd managed to survive the war but not without a severe ordeal. After joining the 15th Alabama at Camp Toombs near Centreville, Virginia, the Confederate army, commanded at that time by General Joseph E. Johnston, went into winter quarters. As the spring of 1862 emerged, the 15th Alabama was assigned to General Stonewall Jackson's command, where the regiment experienced its first real combat. The 15th Alabama became part of the great fighting force described as "Jackson's Foot Cavalry," which defeated three separate Union armies in the famous Shenandoah Valley Campaign of 1862. After constant marching and fighting, Jackson's force, including the 15th Alabama, joined the Army of Northern Virginia under General Robert E. Lee just in time to participate in the Seven Days Campaign, a series of battles fought around Richmond, Virginia, to drive the Union army of the Potomac away from the Confederate capitol.

15th Alabama, Co. E Muster Role for Richard D. Byrd.

On June 29, 1862, the 15th Alabama engaged in the attack on Union forces at the Battle of Gaine's Mill or Old Cold Harbor. This engagement was an important Confederate victory, as General George B. McClellan's Union forces were driven from the field. However, casualties were high in the regiment. Richard Daniel Byrd was seriously wounded in the charge that broke the Union line. A cousin, George Byrd of Company G, was killed.[56]

Richard D. recovered from his wounds and rejoined his regiment. But, his condition required that he be assigned often to teamster duty.[57] The 15th Alabama went on to

---

56   General Thomas Jonathan Jackson became known as "Stonewall" during the Battle of 1st Manassas when troops rallied around him as he sat on his horse like a stonewall as bullets flew all around him. Jackson's army became known as the foot cavalry because of the speed they marched. A complete history of the 15th Alabama Infantry Regiment is Oates, General William C., *The War Between the Union and the Confederacy and its Lost Opportunities with a History of the 15th Alabama Regiment and the Forty-Eight Battles in Which it was Engaged* (1905). The Neale Publishing Co., New York and Washington. This book contains a description on page 116 by Private William McClendon of the attack at Gaine's Mill in which Richard D. Byrd was wounded and a cousin was killed. William C. Oates commanded the 15th Alabama for most of its history. He was born in Pike County and lived in Abbeville and Eufaula after the Civil War. Also, Oates became a US Congressman and was Governor of Alabama. His book is one of the most cited pieces of Civil War literature.

57   See Oates, William C., *The War Between the Union and the Confederacy*, p. 634.

become one of the most decorated Confederate regiments of the war. It was involved in almost every key engagement of the Army of Northern Virginia until Lee's surrender at Appomattox. The one exception was the Battle of Chancellorsville when the 15th Alabama was reassigned from Stonewall Jackson's corps command to General James Longstreet's corps and sent south below Richmond on a foraging expedition for new supplies. The 15th was combined with other Alabama regiments into a new brigade under General Evander Law. Law's brigade was merged into General John Bell Hood's division of Longstreet's corp.[58]

After the Battle of Gettysburg in which the 15th Alabama played a key heroic role, Longstreet's corps, including the 15th, was sent west to temporarily join with the Confederate Army of Tennessee under General Braxton Bragg in an effort to defeat the Union army commanded by General William S. Rosecrans located near Chattanooga, Tennessee. The combination led to the Battle of Chickamauga in

---

58   In addition to General Oates' comprehensive history of the 15th Alabama, a useful history of Company E., Richard D. Byrd's unit, is available at The Men of Co. E, 15th Alabama Infantry Regiment CSA, http://www.flemingmultimedia.com/15thAlaCoE. Also, an excellent book about the brigade containing the 15th Alabama for most of its combat history is Laine, J. Gary and Penny, Morris M. *Law's Alabama Brigade in the War Between the Union and the Confederacy* (1996) White Mane Publishing Co., Shippensburg, Pennsylvania.

northwest Georgia and produced the greatest Confederate victory in the western theatre of the war. Following the battle, General Longstreet took his two divisions, which included the 15th Alabama, and marched toward Knoxville, Tennessee in order to defeat Union forces under General Ambrose Burnside and open eastern Tennessee to Confederate control. The campaign turned into a stalemate and the 15th Alabama went into winter quarters around Dandridge and Mossy Creek. On January 2, 1864, Richard Daniel Byrd was captured while serving as a forage guard during a patrol to gather supplies and food.[59]

Richard D. was sent with other captives from similar patrols to Louisville, Kentucky and then on to Rock Island Prison Camp in Illinois. By this stage of the war, prisoner exchanges were rare and so he spent the rest of the conflict as a POW. Richard D. was paroled on February 22, 1865 after pledging allegiance to the United States when it was obvious the end of the Confederacy was near.[60]

---

59   See Laine, J. Gary and Penny, Morris M., *Law's Alabama Brigade*, pp. 208–217.

60   Richard Daniel Byrd's prisoner of war roll card can be found in the National Archives, Index to Compiled Service Records of Confederate Soldiers. Richard's parole card is illustrated in this text and can also be found in the National Archives Index.

Parole card for Richard D Byrd from Rock Island, Illinois POW compound.

After enlisting in Ozark, Newton Tack Byrd caught up with the 33rd Alabama near Murfreesboro, Tennessee. On September 20, 1863, Tack found himself involved with many of his cousins of Company I in the opening assault at the Battle of Chickamauga. The 33rd Alabama was part of General Patrick Cleburne's division. This division was regarded as the best combat unit in the Army of Tennessee. General Cleburne was a first-generation Irish immigrant and was nicknamed the "Stonewall of the West." The attack by Cleburne's division was met with huge resistance, but the Confederate line held firm and caused enough concern at Union headquarters that reinforcements were ordered to be taken from defensive positions. This shift created a weak spot in the Union defense just as General Longstreet's divisions—including the 15th Alabama and Richard Daniel Byrd—launched their attack. This assault broke through the Union line and created a panic-stricken retreat leading to Confederate victory. While Tack Byrd survived his first battle, the 33rd Alabama suffered a sixty percent casualty rate.[61]

---

61   Much of the 33rd Alabama's history is part of the history of Major General Patrick R. Cleburne's Infantry Division in the Army of Tennessee. An excellent book about this division and the life of Patrick R. Cleburne is Symonds, Craig L., *Stonewall of the West* (1997) University Press of Kansas, Lawrence, Kansas. For an account of the 33rd Alabama's involve-

33rd Alabama Infantry Regiment Co. I Muster Role for Newton Byrd.

ment in the Battle of Chickamauga see pages 147–149. The 33rd Alabama suffered a sixty percent casualty rate in this engagement.

The 33rd went on to further glory with Patrick Cleburne, fighting at Missionary Ridge and the entire Atlanta campaign. However, after General John Bell Hood took over command of the Army of Tennessee from General Joseph E. Johnston, his aggressive tactics with an outnumbered force significantly depleted its strength and morale. By the time General Hood marched his struggling army to Franklin, Tennessee on November 29, 1864, his reputation as an army commander was destroyed. Only a strong sense of patriotic duty remained with the surviving soldiers, especially in Patrick Cleburne's division. Along with Tack Byrd, only two close cousins were left in I Company of the 33rd; Curtis Byrd and Elisha Edward Byrd.[62]

Many Civil War historians have written that General Hood's ordered attack at Franklin across a vast open plain against a strong Union defensive position was an act of exhausted desperation and possibly psychosomatic blood lust. It was the end of Hood's army as a fighting force. Cleburne's division, including the 33rd Alabama, led the charge that Cleburne himself knew was the end. He personally led his men into battle and had two horses shot from under him, then proceeded on foot and was shot through the

---

62   See Symonds, Craig L., *Stonewall of the West*, pp. 242–253.

heart as he approached the Union defenses. The 33rd Alabama charged on through the first line of Union trenches and was finally halted in hand-to-hand combat at the second line of defense.

Unable to retreat without being shot down from behind, the remains of Company I held on in front of the wall-like barricades until they were either dead or captured. Newton Tack Byrd and his two cousins were taken prisoner. Curtis Byrd also lost his arm in the vicious fighting. Newton was sent to Camp Douglas in Chicago, Illinois, where John R. Johnson had died in 1862, to wait out the end of the war. Although this prison was notoriously brutal, he made it home. Curtis and Elisha Edward survived their imprisonment at other locations and also returned home.[63]

63　See Symonds, Craig L., *Stonewall of the West*, pp. 254–260. Other good accounts of General Hood's behavior and the Confederate attack at Franklin, Tennessee are: McMurry, Richard M., *John Bell Hood and the War for Southern Independence* (1982) University Press of Kentucky. Lexington, Kentucky, pp. 174–176; Foote, Shelby, *The Civil War: A Narrative* (1974) Random House, New York, pp. 666–675. Newton Tack Byrd's prisoner of war role card is illustrated in this text and can be found in the *National Archives, Index to Compiled Service Records of Confederate Soldiers*.

Prisoner of War roll from Union army headquarters in Nashville, Tennessee for Newton Byrd captured at the Battle of Franklin.

In some ways, Dale County, Alabama was fortunate. It was not an area constantly fought over with the ebb and flow of vast armies like Virginia or Georgia. So, the land and buildings were manageable. But surviving soldiers and their families still had to face a devastated economy and years of repressive reconstruction policies. Life would go on in an atmosphere of proud impoverishment.

When Newton Tack Byrd was discharged from Camp Douglas on June 6, 1865, he had become a hardened young man. Yet, he was still only nineteen years old. It was time to turn swords to plow shares. After returning home to Dale County, he married Sarah L. Deloney and they began to build a family of five boys and two girls. The 1870 US Census shows that by this time, Tack and Sarah had two children—Winston, who was one year old and Charles (Charlie), who was only a baby. Tack's assets were estimated to be worth about $600. By the 1880 US Census, Tack and Sarah's family had grown to four; Winston, Charles, Emma, and Jesse. During the 1880s, Tack built a new house at their farm on what is now County Road 223. This house still stands and remains in the family to this day. By 1890, their family was complete with the addition of David, Marietta, and finally Edward, who had been born a year earlier.

*Newton Tack Byrd, Sarah Deloney Byrd, and Jesse Byrd (on the carriage)
in front of their new house, 1880s.*

Sarah Deloney Byrd would live only three more years; she died on February 15, 1893 at the relatively early age of forty-eight. Tack continued on alone for almost five years, farming his land and raising the children. Both Winston and Charles had already left the family to make their own way, but they remained in the area so they could still help out at times. Jesse and David were too young for major responsibilities yet. On September 16, 1897, Tack married Mary Smith from another local family. Mary was born in 1859 and was fourteen years younger than Tack. Tack was fifty-two years old at the time of their marriage and she was thirty-eight. There is no record that they had any children together. Tack and Mary were still together when the 1910 census was taken and it appears that the only other person in the household was Tack's son Jesse, who was thirty years old. Mary died a few years later after a sudden stroke. Tack eventually moved from the farm to stay with his son David F. Byrd until his death on March 20, 1926.[64]

---

64   See the US Census, 1870, Ozark District, Newton Byrd, no. 32. This was the last federal census to ask the question and estimate personal and real estate assets. See the US Census, 1880, Ozark District, Newton Byrd, no. 13. The house Tack Byrd built in the 1880s is illustrated in this text along with Tack himself, his wife Sarah, and Jesse. This house is still in the family today. It is owned by my first cousin, Joan Johnson.

See the Alabama Marriage Index, Vol. D which documents the marriage of Newton Byrd and Mary Smith.

See the US Census, 1910, Ozark District, Newton Byrd, no. 10.

David F. Byrd, Tack's son, was a close friend of my grandfather Robert L. Jordan on my mother's side of the family. Robert L. Jordan wrote an intimate memorial obituary in the local newspaper when David F. Byrd died September 7, 1941. Robert L. and David F. were both devout Primitive Baptists and held official positions in the church. This relationship likely added favor to my father, David F. Byrd's nephew, when he courted my mother. It also helped that my mother's best friend was Sara Byrd Flowers, the daughter of David F. Byrd and his wife Etta Lee Peters Byrd.

Gravestones for Newton Tack Byrd and Sarah Deloney Byrd at Hopeful Church cemetery.

When Richard Daniel Byrd was paroled from Rock Island POW Camp in 1865, he returned home to Alabama and made good on his promise to John R. Johnson to take care of his wife Sarah Whittington Johnson and daughter Mary if John were to die in the war. Richard D. married Sarah on January 3, 1868. Sarah and Richard had four children together: Bovine, Sarah Elizabeth, Benjamin, and Mattie.

Data from the 1870 Census indicate that Richard D. owned a farm in the Westville area of Dale County and his assets were valued at about $900. Westville was absorbed into Fort Rucker when it was created in the 1940s. By 1880, Richard D. and Sarah's family was complete. Step-daughter Mary Johnson Byrd was now twenty-one years old and still part of the household.[65] While it seems that Mary was accepted within Richard D.'s new family with her mother Sarah, clinical studies clearly show that alienation and loneliness can easily set in with an older, single step-child, especially if the natural mother becomes more focused on her new family. Also, still being a single young woman at twenty-one in 1880 could carry a lot of pressure to make something happen. But for whatever reason, Mary had a child out of wedlock. Henderson Franklin Johnson was born April 29, 1883. He was my grandfather and he turned out to be one of the kindest, most respected men of Dale County, Alabama. As he was growing up, Henderson seems to have been well liked. He is commonly included in photographs with Richard Daniel Byrd's family.[66]

---

65   See the US Census, 1870, Westville District, R.D. Byrd, no. 42. See the US Census, 1880, Westville District, no. 31.

66   While it is probably unrealistic to apply the results of modern psychological studies to a situation that was one of the most, if not the most, traumatic periods in American history, such analysis might still prove useful as a benchmark for what might be expected in a more prosperous, lower-risk environment. Almost all studies of adolescent female children with step parents show a much higher likelihood of behavior

Mary Johnson Byrd in her late teens or early 20s—about 1880.

problems, reduced future economic prospects, and children out of wed-lock. See a summary of such research in "Children in Step Families: Negative Consequences," Marriage blog, www.wingnutwatch.typepad.com, October 18, 2015.

Henderson Franklin Johnson's birthdate is recorded on his World War I Draft Registration card, serial number 311, order number 355, September 12, 1918. Henderson's natural father is still unknown to this date.

Photographs of Henderson Franklin Johnson with the family of Richard Daniel Byrd are contained in Averett, *Byrd History*, p. 465. The clarity of the images was not strong enough to reproduce in this book.

Richard Daniel Byrd—1880s.

Sarah Whittington Johnson Byrd—1880s.

Gravestones of Sarah Whittington Johnson Byrd and Richard Daniel Byrd at Enterprise City Cemetery.

On September 26, 1885, Marietta Byrd was born to Newton Tack and Sarah Deloney Byrd. She was always referred to as "Shug" and was the youngest daughter in the family. Marietta and Henderson Johnson were roughly the same age. They knew each other from childhood since Tack Byrd and Richard Daniel Byrd were cousins and shared the brotherhood of common war experiences. In addition, both families lived in close proximity to each other. Richard D.'s farm was near Westville just down the road from Tack's farm near Hopeful Church. Also, on December 20, 1892, Mary Johnson Byrd married Henry Sellers, whose farm was adjacent to the farm of Curtis Byrd (Richard D.'s brother) and very near Richard D.'s farm. Henderson Johnson was nine years old at the time and Marietta was seven.

My grandfather, Henderson Franklin Johnson (at 15) standing behind his mother, Mary Johnson Byrd Sellers (far right), Henry Sellers (center), Bovine Byrd Andrews (far left) and young children Randall and Vera Sellers, 1898.

Henderson and Marietta were a close pair by the time they decided to marry at Hopeful Church on December 24, 1905. It was only natural that eventually members of the Byrd and Johnson clans would get together, especially with a Johnson so intertwined with the Byrds as Henderson Franklin. After all, the Byrds and Johnsons had left North Carolina together in the same wagon train and entered Dale County, Alabama together in 1828. Also, there was already an important early precedent when Acrel Byrd, son of Bright, and original pioneer brother with Redding, married Bartilla Johnson back in 1841.

Soon after their marriage, Henderson was able to acquire land just south of Tack Byrd's farm along what is now Route 27. They raised their family there and lived in the same house for the rest of their lives. Marietta and Henderson's first child died in infancy. Their second child and senior son born October 15, 1910 was my father Manuel Holman Johnson. He was followed by four other brothers: Howard, Travis, Paul, and Lamar.[67]

---

67   Mary Johnson Byrd's marriage to Henry Sellers is recorded in the Alabama Marriage Index, 1800–1969. The marriage was performed by W.W. Morris.

Marietta Byrd's marriage to Henderson Franklin Johnson is recorded in the Alabama Marriage Index, 1814–1935. The marriage was performed by D.F. Byrd.

According to my father and uncles, Marietta Byrd Johnson was a wonderful, loving mother. Tragically, she did not survive long after bearing her sons and seeing her oldest reach nineteen and the youngest just eleven. She died after an extended illness on March 14, 1930 and was buried just up the road at Hopeful Church cemetery. Marietta was only forty-five.

Henderson Franklin Johnson only lived another five years after Marietta's death. He died on May 20, 1935 after contracting gangrene from a leg infection. He was buried at Hopeful Church cemetery beside Marietta. Henderson was only fifty-two.

According to the obituary of Acrel Byrd in Averett, *Byrd History*, p. 918, Acrel married Bartilla Johnson in 1841.

Regarding the five sons of Marietta and Henderson: Howard died young due to an accident while working in Florida; Manuel Sr., Travis Sr., and Lamar served in the military during World War II, all making it home safely. Of the surviving four brothers, Lamar, the youngest, died in his seventies, but the others lived into their eighties.

*Marietta 'Shug' Byrd
in 1905 at age 20.*

Henderson Franklin Johnson, 1920.

In his relatively short life, Henderson became a successful farmer and supervised many livestock auctions in Ozark. He was so respected by his friend Henry Steagall, the 3rd Alabama district congressman and chairman of the US House Banking Committee, that he was invited several times to testify before the US Congress on livestock grading and auction regulatory policy. He was also instrumental in helping US officials decide on establishing a federal government development project on Byrd traditional lands when the Great Depression was impoverishing the country. This area eventually became the Fort Rucker military reservation.[68]

---

68   According to the US Census, 1910, Ozark Precinct, Henderson F. Johnson, no. 213, Marietta and Henderson had one child that was no longer living.

In 1933, Henderson Franklin Johnson testified before the US House of Representatives Agriculture Committee regarding the impact of livestock auction policies and procedures on producer and consumer prices. He delivered his testimony on this same subject before the US Senate Agriculture Committee the same week.

For an overview of Henderson Franklin Johnson's involvement in the early development of Fort Rucker military reservation, see McGee, Val L., The Origin of Fort Rucker (1987) The Dale County Historical Society, Inc., Ozark, Alabama, pp. 15–29. Also see "Honoring and Preserving the Heritage: An Architectural History of Ozark, 1824–1957" Dale County Historical Society video disc.

As a bit of irony, Congressman Henry B. Steagall became the powerful chairman of the House Banking and Finance Committee in 1930 and

Henderson Franklin Johnson and Marietta Byrd Johnson, 1925.

was the co-author with Virginia Senator Carter Glass of the 1933 Glass-Steagall Act. This legislation primarily prevented affiliations between banks and securities firms as a result of the concerns about bank collapses and the stock market crash. When I became Vice Chairman of the Federal Reserve Board in 1986, times were changing and banks were innovatively getting around the restrictions on underwriting securities using loopholes in the law. I found myself working to bring an end to Henry Steagall's legacy by supporting measures to restructure the banking laws consistent with the original intent but up to date with modern reality. I kept seeing my grandfather in my sleep asking why I was attacking his dear friend.

Gravestones of Henderson Franklin Johnson and Marietta Byrd Johnson at Hopeful Church Cemetery.

Manuel Holman Johnson Sr., 1930.

Families of the sons of Henderson Franklin Johnson and Marietta Byrd Johnson. From left: Paul, Henderson, Ree, Travis Sr., Travis Jr., Martha Jo, Mary Holman, Manuel Jr., Ethel, Dell, David, and Lamar, 1949.

The four sons of Henderson Franklin Johnson and Marietta Byrd Johnson with grandson Manuel Jr. in the center. From left: Travis, Paul, Manuel Jr., Manuel Sr., and Lamar, 1989.

CHAPTER IV

RETURN TO VIRGINIA

As I stated at the beginning of this genealogical study, Byrd blood runs deep in my family. Ten generations of Byrds from the earliest days of colonial development to this very date make this proud family line as steeped in American history as one can imagine. On a final note, it seemed like fate to me when my family moved to Virginia in the 1970s, the place where it all began for the Byrds in America. Later, when I was nominated to be Assistant Secretary of the US Treasury by President Ronald Reagan in 1982, I knew it was fate when I was sponsored and introduced to the US Senate Finance Committee for my confirmation hearing by Senator Harry F. Byrd, Jr. in his last official act before retiring from the Senate.[69]

---

69   See Hearing Before the Committee of Finance United States Senate, 97th Congress, 2nd session on nominations of Susan W. Liebeler and Enrique J. Leon to be Commissioners of the International Trade Commission and Manuel H. Johnson, Jr. to be Assistant Secretary of the Treasury, December 8, 1982, US Government Printing Office, Washington, DC, 1983.

The cover of this hearing document and Senator Harry F. Byrd Jr.'s introductory statement are illustrated in the text.

NOMINATIONS OF MANUEL H. JOHNSON, JR., SUSAN W. LIEBELER AND ENRIQUE J. LEON

HEARING

BEFORE THE

COMMITTEE ON FINANCE
UNITED STATES SENATE

NINETY-SEVENTH CONGRESS

SECOND SESSION

ON

NOMINATIONS OF

SUSAN W. LIEBELER AND ENRIQUE J. LEON TO BE COMMISSIONERS OF THE INTERNATIONAL TRADE COMMISSION AND MANUEL H. JOHNSON, JR., TO BE ASSISTANT SECRETARY OF THE TREASURY

———————

DECEMBER 8, 1982

———————

Printed for the use of the Committee on Finance

U.S. GOVERNMENT PRINTING OFFICE

14-376 O   WASHINGTON : 1983   HG 97-127

Record of Senate Confirmation Hearing for Manuel Holman Johnson Jr., 1982.

The CHAIRMAN. I think what we would like to do now is just take a few minutes and Senator Byrd would introduce Manuel H. Johnson, who has been nominated to be an Assistant Secretary of the Treasury. I think we can dispose—I don't mean it in that sense—but we can act, we can handle this nomination fairly rapidly, and then move on to the gas tax.

Senator Byrd?

Senator BYRD. Thank you, Mr. Chairman.

Manuel H. Johnson of Virginia has been nominated for the important position of Assistant Secretary of the Treasury for Economic Policy. Mr. Johnson is a native of Alabama. He took his Ph. D. degree from Florida State University. He was in the department of economics of that university and then he came to Virginia as assistant professor and then associate professor of economics. George Mason University is an outstanding university, and while I do not know Mr. Johnson well, my understanding is that he made an outstanding record at George Mason University as associate professor of economics. More recently he has been Deputy Assistant Secretary for Economic Policy in the Treasury Department, and now has been nominated to be Assistant Secretary for Economic Policy.

I am delighted to present Manuel H. Johnson to this committee and to commend him to you for swift approval of his nomination. Thank you.

The CHAIRMAN. Thank you, Senator Byrd.

Introduction of Manuel Holman Johnson Jr. for Senate Confirmation Hearing by Senator Harry F. Byrd, Jr., from the Congressional Record.

Senator Harry F. Byrd, Jr. began his career in the US Senate after his father Harry F. Byrd, Sr., the longest serving Virginian in history, resigned his seat for health reasons in 1965. Harry, Jr. was initially appointed by Virginia governor Albertis Harrison to serve in his father's place until the next general election. After winning election to a full senate term in 1966, he went on to serve a second full term ending with his retirement at the beginning of the senate class of 1983. [70]

Harry, Jr.'s retirement from the US Senate ended the greatest political dynasty in the long history of Virginia. For the previous eighty years, a Byrd of the Westover line had held important public office. After taking over his father's struggling newspaper in Winchester at the age of fifteen and making it successful by implementing a pay-as-you-go policy, Harry Flood Byrd, Sr. employed this frugal financial philosophy to everything he touched. As a result, he became a prospering businessman and gained a loyal following that supported him for election to the Virginia state senate in 1915 at the age of 28. By 1925, he was governor of Virginia and in 1933 he was first appointed and then elected to the US Senate, an office he would hold by popular demand until his health gave out in 1965.[71]

---

70 See Hatch, Alden, *The Byrds of Virginia: An American Dynasty, 1670 to the Present*, p.516.

71 See Hatch, Alden, *The Byrds of Virginia*, pp. 401-520.

Appendix B illustrates the family tree of Harry F. Byrd Sr. and Harry F. Byrd Jr. published in an article on the Byrds of Virginia by Time magazine, August, 17, 1972, p.13

Senator Harry Flood Byrd Sr.   *Senator Harry Flood Byrd Jr.*

"Rosemont" former home of Senator Harry Flood Byrd Sr. in Berryville, Virginia.

As I have pointed out earlier, my Byrd line was known for its frugality and culture of living modestly within ones means. My father Manuel H. Johnson, Sr. (always referred to as Holman) was a classic example of this genetic trait. Holman Johnson was never known to incur a single dollar of debt in his entire lifetime. He never owned a credit card, only a pay-as-you-go card. After moving to Virginia with my wife, Mary, in 1977 and holding public office as Assistant Treasury Secretary for Economic Policy for four years, I was nominated by President Ronald Reagan to serve as governor and then vice chairman of the Federal Reserve Board in 1986. My parents, sisters, and in-laws traveled to Washington, DC to attend my swearing in ceremony at the Federal Reserve Headquarters on Constitution Avenue. At the time, Paul Volcker was chairman of the Board of Governors. Paul was renowned for his tight-fisted financial and monetary policies. After my swearing in, Chairman Volker pulled me aside during the reception and explained that he had just finished a conversation with my father. He said that until this discussion, he thought he was the stingiest man in America, but now he discovered he was second to my father.

Swearing in ceremony with Manuel Holman Johnson Jr, family, and Paul Volker.

Probably because I did not live through the Great Depression in the 1930s like my father and both Harry Byrd, Sr. and Jr., I did not have the same abhorrence of debt that they possessed. Trained as an economist, I always evaluated debt on a cost/benefit basis, but I certainly understood and appreciated their culture of financial prudence. Like my Byrd ancestors, I was known for promoting conservative fiscal policies that emphasized federal spending restraint and the requirement of financial discipline. These are characteristics that I have always believed in and follow in my personal affairs to this day. I have urged this philosophy to my children who are now responsible adults.

My wife, Mary, and I have now lived in Virginia for almost forty years. Our children Marshall and Merritt were born and raised here. We reside much of the year at our country home, Holman Hall, in Upperville, just a stone's throw from Rosemont in Berryville where Harry F. Byrd, Sr. held court and Courtfield in Winchester, the former home of Harry F. Byrd, Jr. We also love our Alabama roots. We were both born and raised in Troy, Pike County, Alabama, a wonderful community not far from my father's Ozark, Dale County, origins. I will always be grateful for my Byrd family background and try to live up to the high standards set by my ancestors.

"Holman Hall" home of Manuel Holman Johnson Jr. in Upperville, Virginia.

Appendix A

Genealogy
The Byrds in England

1. HUGH LE BIRD, younger son of the family of Charlton, m. Werburga, daughter of Roger Dombvel, and had issue: 2. John, m. Isabel—, and had a son, Hugh le Bird, who d. s. p. ; 3. Richard; 4. William, m., and had a son, John le Bird, who d. s. p.

3. Richard, m. Mary, daughter of Henry Brentishall, and had a son,

5. David, m. Elizabeth, daughter of John Fitzhugh, of Lithrogg, and had a son,

6. Hugh, m. Roose, daughter of Albaney Cheyney, and had a son,

7. David, m. Mabel, sister and heir of Henry de Broxton, and had issue: 8. Richard; 9. Hugh; and 10. William, about whom there is no data.

8. Richard le Bird, of Broxton, m. Mabel Codogan, and had a son, 11. Hugh.

9. Hugh le Bird, m. Agnes, daughter of William de Bickerton, and had issue: 12. David of Broxton; 13. Ughtred, who left two sons, Thomas and David; 14. John, of Broxton.

11. Hugh le Bird, m. —, and had a son, John le Bird of Broxton, whose daughter and heiress was Margaret, who in 1379 was wife of Roger Bulkeley.

12. David le Bird, of Broxton, m. Mawde, daughter of David de Edge, of Edge and had a son,

15. John Bird, m. Alice, daughter and heiress of Peter Bulkeley, of Broxton (by his wife Nicola, daughter of Thomas Bird), and had issue: 16. John (who witnessed a deed in 1440 and had a son, John le Bird, of Tilston, who was living in 1467); 17. Tomalyn.

17. Tomalyn Bird, of Bostock, living in 1440, m. Phillippa, daughter of Hugh Broxton, of Henhall, and had a son,

18. Henry Bird, of Broxton, m. Winifred, daughter and heiress of Adam de Raley, and had a son,

19. John le Bird, of Broxton, m. Ciceley, daughter of John Dutton, of Hatton, and had issue: 20. Peter; 21. Thomas; 22. John.

20. Peter le Bird, of Broxton, m. Anne, daughter of Richard Clive, of Clive, and had a son, George le Bird, of Broxton, who m. Elizabeth, daughter of David Dodd, of Edge, and in turn had a son, Thomas, who m. Jane, daughter of Ralph Bulkeley, of Haughton. (Here in Holm's pedigree this branch of the family ends.)

21. Thomas le Bird, m. Margaret, daughter of William Dodd, of Broxton, and had a son,

23. Henry le Bird, of Broxton, m. Anne, daughter of John Phelkin, of Tattenhall, and had issue: 24. John; 25. Thomas; 26. Hughe (d.s.p.); 27. Robert; 28. Roger; 29. Anne, m. John Carden, of Calcott; 30. Elizabeth m. Hugh Williamson, of Chalkley; 31. Mary, m. Richard Davenport, of Locroff; 32. Katherine; 33. Robert, m. Elizabeth, daughter of Francis Lolland (or Callorne), of Aymount.

24. John le Bird, of London, m. Elizabeth, daughter of Oliver Burgh als Copparsmith, and had issue: (a) William; (b) John; (c) Henry; (d) Elizabeth; (e) Anne.

25. Thomas le Bird, m. Ales Palyn, and had issue: (f) Anne; (g) Raphe; (h) Margery; (i) Peter; (j) Jane; (k) Thomas.

27. Robert Bird, m. Elizabeth Holland, and had a son,

34. John Bird, m. Elizabeth Bine, and had a son,

35. Thomas Bird, m. Elizabeth Bird, and had issue: 36. John; 37. William.

36. John Bird, or Byrd, of London. He was a goldsmith of London, m. Grace, daughter of Thomas Stegg, or Stegge, of London (and for a time of Virginia, where he held important office), and had issue: 38. William, eldest son, and founder of the family in Virginia; 39. Thomas, who was perhaps the youngest child; and four daughters: Elizabeth (who perhaps m. Rand), Mary (who perhaps m. Guy), and Sarah and Grace (one of who perhaps m. Robinson).

This genealogy was taken from Holme's "Heraldic Collections for Chester" (Harleian MSS., No. 2119), and from a pedigree prepared at the Heralds' College, London, in 1702, for William Byrd. Some of the facts in this genealogy have been updated for information discovered in more recent research . See Stewart, "The First William Bird of Charles City County, Virginia," The Virginia Magazine of History and Biography, Vol. 41, No. 3 (July, 1933), pp. 189-195.

Appendix B

Family Tree of Harry F. Byrd Sr. and Jr.

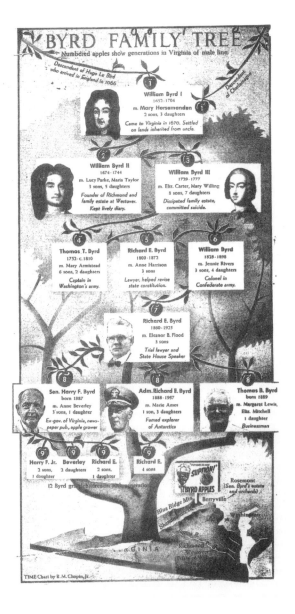

INDEX

C